T0198411

Marisol's
Brand-New Feet

MARIA TERESA ALCOCER

Copyright © 2021 by Maria Teresa Alcocer. 816305

All rights reserved. No part of this book may be reproduced or transmitted in any form or by any means, electronic or mechanical, including photocopying, recording, or by any information storage and retrieval system, without permission in writing from the copyright owner.

The views expressed in this work are solely those of the author and do not necessarily reflect the views of the publisher, and the publisher hereby disclaims any responsibility for them.

To order additional copies of this book, contact:
Xlibris
844-714-8691
www.Xlibris.com
Orders@Xlibris.com

ISBN: Softcover   978-1-6641-6293-8
         EBook   978-1-6641-6292-1

Print information available on the last page

Rev. date: 06/16/2021

Reason for This Book

This testimony was written to help and educate children and families about *talipes equinovarus*. The purpose is to relieve the anxiety during difficult moments that children in so many hospitals and homes in the world are going through at this moment or perhaps like so many who suffer a similar disability.

Endorsement

"Maria Teresa Alcocer has devoted many years to improving the quality of life of young and old. She has taught literature to children and adults with the intent of opening their eyes to the beauty expressed by the written word. Her stories are surprisingly simple; they speak to all of us."

—Dr. Sieg Hirsch

Sometimes in life, it is not just fate that shapes our destiny but also the many helping, comforting hands that help shape that destiny—in this case, for a little girl named Marisol.

—Maria Teresa Alcocer

Dedication

*With all my love
for
Tommy, Samira, Rania, Lucas, Isabella, Ava, Edward, Anakin, Madelaine, Deeann,
Sofia, Jack, Rio, and Marcelo*

Gratitude

My immense gratitude and special thanks to my family; doctors; nurses;
close friends; the Rotary Clubs in Cochabamba, Bolivia, and Van Nuys,
California; and the OASIS Writers Group in San Antonio, Texas.

To My Godchild Marisol

Maria Teresa Alcocer

My dear godchild,
the day I met you, you owned my heart.
Your gaze and sweet smile remained in my mind.
I have loved you from the start.
I was compelled by compassion, feeling that would not go away.
I knew I had a mission. The thought to help correct an imperfection came to mind.
I could not be indifferent. *We must always be of service*, I thought.
You needed love, care, and it was the right time to lend a hand.
Good actions and small deeds are opportunities that one must take.
You stayed deep in my heart.
You are not just another girl; you are a child of God.
I am glad I heard my heart's call. You filled my life with lots of fun.
Sometimes our journey was hard, with lots of pain,
heartaches, tears, and sleepless nights.
Things were not easy, but time is a healer.
You stayed deep in my heart.
I am thankful for the time we spent. It all went by—slowly or fast.
At last came the day, the awaited moment—
when I held your hand so you could take
your first steps with your brand-new feet with care!
Oh … that day we embraced and cried with joy.
You stayed deep in my heart.
Today all fear is gone.
All is in the past, and you are not feeling lonely or sad.
Your feet are straight; now you can folk dance to your heart's content,
and no one can say, "You cannot join a dance."

The little girl looked up at me with her sad eyes, then downward to her feet. It was like her gaze was saying to me, "Please take a look at my feet." Little did I know at that moment that this little girl and her story were going to change my life in a way I would have never imagined.

Marisol was the name of the little girl. In learning more about her life, I found out that she was born to a very humble family. Her place of birth was near the rainforest in the state of Beni, Bolivia, South America. What made Marisol so special was her feet. She was born with feet that looked vastly different from the other children in her small town.

The medical condition she was born with is called *bilateral clubfoot*. Children born with this congenital deformity have feet that are hard to move, being rigid and inverted. The feet are rotated internally at the ankles and pointed down, and the soles face each other. The scientific term is called *talipes equinovarus*. According to the National Institute of Health (NIH), one in every thousand infants is born with clubfoot.

Babies born with clubfeet can potentially live a perfectly ordinary life. Sadly, this was not to be the case for Marisol. Her mother, being a teenager when she gave birth to Marisol, listened to the almost primitive treatment the local physicians recommended in treating her baby's clubfeet deformity. One of the doctors proceeded to treat the infant's syndrome with splinting—using boards and bandages to straighten out the deformity. This medical correction turned out to be futile because of the pain and discomfort, that the splints were affecting her daily life.

Any normal baby learns to walk independently; however, in Marisol's case, it was practically impossible to have learned how to do so. Due to her incapacity, she was constantly carried by her parents, and she did not learn to be autonomous until much later.

One day, shortly after her fourth birthday, she surprised her family by dragging her body forward and pulling herself upright on the furniture. That day she took her first very awkward steps, making everybody so happy. Gradually she learned to stand up on her ankles and use them as her body's support and just began to walk.

Marisol never thought she was different from the other children. She was a joyful little girl. She seemed totally unaware of her physical limitations due to her disability— perhaps being too young to be aware or perhaps being too spirited for it to make a difference to her. At some point, one would have to wonder whether this little girl was so comfortable with her condition that she might even be opposed to being made "normal" by having her situation treated and surgically corrected.

By the time Marisol turned six, she was energetic, outgoing, and free as a butterfly. She loved climbing and jumping down from trees. She swam in the river and did cartwheels, possibly even when she felt pain. She had an extremely competitive little spirit, always wanting to do what other children her age were doing, not ever wanting to be left behind.

When it was time for her to attend school, Marisol and her oldest sister walked many blocks to catch the local bus that took them to a street corner near their school. Marisol's life at that point was not easy or very carefree. Even though she loved school and learning, most days were not happy ones. She experienced bullying, not only by the students in her grade but also sadly by the very teachers who were there to educate her. Equally, the whole school system endorsed this behavior in their educators.

Marisol had a desire to participate in the traditional folkloric dances and other physical school activities. Possibly because of their lack of compassionate insight, the teachers discouraged her participation, fearful that Marisol's congenital clubfoot condition would make their school look bad. This made Marisol sad and angry but also much more determined to follow her own happiness.

An important turning point in Marisol's life came when her family moved to a bigger city where her parents found work. Miguel, Marisol's father, had been injured in his previous lumber job and was still recovering from this unfortunate accident that almost took his life. Due to his long recovery period, he was terminated by his company, motivating him to relocate his family to a larger city.

When Marisol was nine years old, my family came into her life. From the minute we met Marisol, we felt compassion about her disability and her family's situation. We could tell that Marisol was a happy little girl, and her enthusiasm for life could not be ignored. I felt a strong desire to do something to help this child; with this help, she perhaps could lead a more normal and healthy life. Eventually, she could prosper and be afforded the opportunities that had been denied to her for so long.

In my heart of hearts, I felt that Marisol's feet needed to be corrected. I could not imagine her growing up to be a healthy normal teenager with her disability. I knew that I could make a difference in this child's life. I had the means to do so, but mostly I had the strong desire to see how I could help her live a better life. I was confident that healthier and happier moments were ahead for Marisol.

In speaking with Marisol's parents, and then later with Marisol herself, we formed a plan. Her parents and Marisol were immensely grateful and agreed to accept our offer for a medical treatment—therefore help correct her condition, including all that it would entail: the preliminary hospitalization, the surgical intervention, and the physical therapy afterward.

On angels' wings, my prayers went straight to heaven. I prayed to God he would show me a way to help her. This new perspective was the foundation of a reality that a new process of future events had just begun.

During the summer, many of our close friends came to our aid, helping us find the right resources to do this for her. They searched for a trusted children's hospital that specializes and helps children in cases like Marisol's. After a few weeks of investigation, the doors opened and good news arrived at Bolivia that there was a nonprofit children's hospital in the United States that provides specialized care to children with such a condition regardless of the patients' financial needs.

The children's hospital accepted Marisol as an outpatient, and we were told that a preliminary appointment was scheduled for the month of November. They would treat her feet with a method of plaster casting and surgery to correct the imperfection in her tendons, and finally provide the necessary therapy.

All seemed to be going simply fine, then the legal process began. We had to obtain from the local consulate a special medical visa for Marisol and a regular visa for her father, Miguel, who was going to accompany her to travel legally to the United States.

For this to happen, we assigned one of the members of my family to be responsible for escorting and supporting Marisol and her father in all their needs, financially and emotionally. After waiting for a few weeks, an appointment for an official interview at the United States Consulate in La Paz, was scheduled. Fortunately, their request to enter the country was granted. Another milestone was perfectly accomplished in the name of love and service to others.

Several weeks after, on Thanksgiving Day, which was very symbolic indeed, Marisol and her father were finally flying north from La Paz, Bolivia, to Los Angeles, California, in the United States.

Arrival at the Hospital

We arrived at a prestigious children's hospital. It was a wonderful hospital dedicated to helping children. Medical personnel awaited Marisol for her primary doctor's appointment. At dawn, they greeted us with a pleasant welcome. She was nervous as we anxiously waited to be called by a nurse. In the meantime, she watched in amazement the many other children who were also waiting for appointments with doctors. She noticed that some children had even worse disabilities than she did.

At that moment, she started to ask questions about their physical problems. By the look in her face, I was able to see the compassion she felt for them. She realized that she was not alone in her journey to have her feet corrected. She was going to make new friends at the hospital where she was going to be treated.

Marisol's life would soon be changed. Everything was new and different for her. She did not know what to expect, and she was so frightened of the unknown. She was silent most of the time, perhaps thinking what would come next. We must remember that before her treatment, she was still able to walk and dance just fine with her different feet. She did not consider herself handicapped because she had always lived her life as a very normal and active little girl, with only her feet twisted out of position.

Meeting Her Pediatric Orthopedic Surgeon

Marisol met her doctor and the nurses who were going to work hard in her journey to straighten her feet and improve her comfort and function, allowing her to live a more productive normal life.

Everything was pleasant and seemed fine. They were awesomely patient, understanding, and had empathy with the care of her feet and feelings. Still, Marisol was extremely nervous; however, she gradually became more comfortable with their assistance. Besides, her doctor made a lasting impact on her. This feeling changed the entire situation, much more than what I had imagined.

Furthermore, the orthopedic doctor explained to us that they were going to proceed with the following treatment: manipulating, stretching the ligaments, tendons, joint capsules, graphic images, and casting. This corrective method is called Ponseti. Her doctor was going to gradually stretch her feet a few degrees weekly to correct her upward feet. To keep her feet in a corrective position, it was necessary for Marisol to wear a cast that was bent at the knees in a sitting position to accommodate the shape of her pediatric wheelchair. This rigorous treatment needed to be accomplished until her feet reached almost a perfect vertical alignment, allowing her later to stand up straight on planted feet and no longer on her ankles.

At the end of her appointment, it was a little bit sad to hear that this initial treatment required Marisol to be confined to a wheelchair and be unable to walk at all for many months. For this elementary school girl, it was not easy to accept her new way of life because of her energetic personality.

Another factor that would affect Marisol's emotional response to treatment was her father's absence. Although he was present at the beginning of her treatment, he soon had to return to Bolivia to take care of the rest of the family and pending issues. This left Marisol completely under my legal guardianship and under the care of the hospital staff for the remainder of her rigorous treatment.

When visiting the hospital for her weekly appointments, we were able to observe the personnel and the medical institution that specializes in the treatment of pediatric disabilities. There were, and there are, many opportunities were hospitals offer services that provide excellent care for children. At the same time, they allow parents and families to meet their goals. I was so inspired by their genuine compassion and the work that doctors, nurses, and staff members provide. I thought to myself, *Thanks to people like them, our world truly is a better place to live in.*

Marisol's Feelings

On many occasions, Marisol did not know exactly how to express her feelings because of her unfamiliar surroundings and because of my being basically a stranger to her. We both went through challenging moments due to the absence of her parents. It was particularly stressful and upsetting for her. She felt scared and distrustful of the world around her. Sometimes she would become clingy toward me. She, for sure, missed her family back home and often expressed to me, "I am very confused and afraid." I would reply, "Everything is going to be fine. It is only a matter of time. Have faith, and soon all will be part of the past." I knew that being honest with her had helped her to be confident about her own identity. This also gave her a sense of belonging.

What Made Her Most Happy

Marisol felt better after she was able to talk on the telephone with her mother and sisters in Bolivia. Her family was able to bring her comfort just by hearing their voices and for her to relate the events about her first appointment and experience. Marisol's mom would speak to her with a sweet loving voice; she spoke to her softly, telling her always to please be brave, to behave, and to be determined with her cure.

Another important aspect was that many of our friends who lived in the Los Angeles area helped with other issues relating to her health. Others who did not even know her or her abnormality were also able to lend a hand. With their care, company, and compassion, they made possible to continue Marisol's development and medical progress. They praised her bravery and convinced her not to worry about what was to come next. Their kind words, gifts, and support were great. She learned to trust everyone, which helped her to pull her emotions together and keep her spirits up.

Marisol's First Experience at Cast Changing

The discomfort she was struggling with the most, at the beginning was related to the pain she felt by the stretching of her tendons that would gradually correct her feet to make them normal. To control her pain, the doctor prescribed some medication so Marisol would feel continuously comfortable, and thus would be able to sleep better at night. Many times, she had to learn to hold in her emotions and be strong. The fact is that from the top of her legs down to her toes, a cast was placed, which instantly became hard and was changed every week. One of the moments I describe next caused her more stress during her medical care.

Even though Marisol had been previously warned by the nurse not to be afraid of the loud sounds coming from the saw machine, the vacuum cleaner, and the various noisy tools that would be used to remove the hard cast for the first time, all was forgotten; and nonetheless, she became alarmed about the loud noises, which probably sounded like an explosion to her ears. This frightened Marisol so much that she could not contain her tears, her mind deviated, and she had a first scandalous panic attack.

The procedure was simple for the doctor and the nurse. However, to her it was a terror, because she had in mind that the equipment they were using was going to cut off her feet. Apparently, this frame of thinking in Marisol's head came from something her youngest sister, had told her before the trip—that Marisol was going to the United States not to have her feet corrected but to have her feet cut off. That conversation between Marisol and her sister was coming back to stress Marisol out, and it had been said by Lina to steal attention away from her older sister.

That instant, I was glad I was there for her. Her eyes grew wide, and she let out a loud scream. Her arms embraced my neck tightly, she was drenched in sweat and tears, and her mind was racing fast. She imagined terrible things that could happen even though there was no reason that we could see. Moreover, she was feeling unsafe, and she shouted anxiously loud. Clinging from my neck, she would say, "No! No! Please! I do not want them to touch me! They are going to cut my legs off! Oh, please don't let them hurt me!"

I squeezed her in my arms and said, "I promise no one will hurt you. We are here to make your little feet well. I will always protect you and will never allow anyone to hurt you."

Her doctor and nurse understood and respected her fear. To them, this anxious moment was a normal one, one that they had learned to deal with as they treated many patients like Marisol every day. They knew better than to behave perfectly with her first cast-changing experience. They patiently waited for Marisol to calm down. Much composure was needed for Marisol to understand that the weekly casting treatment was all for her benefit. This was not an easy thing for Marisol to comprehend. After all, she was that little girl who had lived in the wilderness all her life, with an almost wild demeanor. She lived in the wilderness in the rainforest of Bolivia, where everything around her was free and practically primitive. Calmness in this strange new environment was a difficult thing for this little girl to grasp.

The nurse and I developed a plan of action for handling her anxiety; the nurse would ask her to take deep breaths, inhaling to a count. I would count out loud to ten and then exhaling to ten. I would ask the nurse to help her not to think the worst and just distract her with trivial conversations about her family and life in Bolivia to calm her down. This gave her the confidence to believe that nothing horrific was happening.

The cast changing was not a big deal. Marisol just needed to understand that the procedure was part of the medical care. We reassured her that all was going to be fine. We even promised her small treats after we were done with the "hard" part of her treatment.

Another treat that the nurse offered Marisol to make her treatment more tolerable was to ask her to choose from a color chart what color of cast she would like to wear that week. On many occasions, Marisol would choose colors to match her outfit. These colors were always attractive ones, either a hot pink, green, turquoise, and candy cane for Christmas. This routine made Marisol incredibly happy; sometimes she'd say, "Um … let me think first. Yes, today I will decide to go with many different colors."

For nine months, these colorful casts were a part of her body. Gradually, with the straightening and cast changes, her feet eventually looked almost normal; often she would say, "They are much better, aren't they, Nina?"

Toward the end of her ten-month outpatient hospital treatment, Marisol became so used to her cast changes that there were no more episodes of tears or anxiety.

In addition, she received gifts—like teddy bears, dolls, blankets, books, beauty boxes, and chocolates—from many of my friends and acquaintances who knew of her plight, followed her progress, and visited her occasionally during her treatment. Marisol was surprised by this outpouring of love from people who were total strangers to her. "Thank you" was her quiet, humble response, but it said it all.

Marisol was smart, sagacious, and a fast learner. She soon was trained to be a self-sufficient little girl. And she soon became an expert in maneuvering her wheelchair around the house, going through doorways and around tight corners, mostly because the house was not designed to be wheelchair accessible.

Toward the end of her treatment, Marisol became quite proficient at navigating her wheelchair with an enthusiasm about her that nothing mattered and she could overcome any barrier, speeding and making turns like a daredevil! "Oops, oops, sorry, sorry" was what she would often say at the beginning. She eventually changed to gleeful laughs as she finally learned to master her wheelchair.

As time passed, Marisol learned to become as independent as she possibly could. For me, it was sad to see Marisol not only confined to a wheelchair but also separated from her family. Mentally I could put myself in Marisol's place. I felt a great deal of responsibility for her. At bedtime, we would have long conversations about her family and how much she missed them all. I'd say, "This might seem like a dream, but I tell you, all will be over soon. I assure you, you will be much better off than before. Time will go by fast." I would then give her a good night kiss and wish her many blessings for a great tomorrow.

Marisol Wears Her Almost New Feet to School

Another major occurrence of importance in Marisol's life was her being able to register for school. Marisol was overly impressed by her new school and the activities in her classes. She was very enthusiastic about making new friends. She was assimilating and learning new concepts to her.

Our daily journey to and from school offered us the opportunity to share our individual activities in life. Marisol kept busy with homework; special projects were her favorite things to do. She learned to speak basic English, which allowed her to become more sociable and to make friends easily.

She was invited to visit some of her school friends for birthday parties or just to spend time away from home, in a different environment. All these activities became to be a part of her healing process and I believe were important.

It seemed that school was one of the best places for her to attend. At the end of the school day, we would greet each other with a big smile. Marisol was very capable and was a fast learner, and she became such a good student. Her grades were superb due to the daily study skills that were instilled at home. She frequently demonstrated her gratitude.

On many occasions, she would say, "I am so happy and excited because I met so many wonderful teachers and friends and I am learning so much." Then she would continue relating her experiences at school.

Families Are Important

Marisol patiently waited for a new week to come and go, and I never underestimated the importance that sharing the news with others is so much fun. Therefore, I need to emphasize that what Marisol enjoyed the most was our phone calls to Bolivia so she could speak with her family on the weekends. She would tell them how much she was missing them. We kept them abreast about the progression of her treatment. She joyfully related to her siblings happy times when our friends would take her sightseeing in Los Angeles to see places that interested her.

On a special occasion, we visited the oceanfront. She was mesmerized by so much water because Bolivia is a landlocked country. Sadly, Bolivia does not have any coastline at all. There are forty-nine countries in the world like Bolivia that are known to be landlocked, having no access to the sea.

She would say to her sisters, "We went to the see the ocean with its huge beach, but the water was cold. I liked it very much, and the feeling of the water and sand in my hands and fingers was superb. You should see. The waves are foamy, tall, and loud."

As days and weeks went by, things became a routine for us. Marisol and I got along well. Medically there had been considerable progress, which made me happy. The accomplishments with her treatment kept our spirits up.

There were still a few more months, weeks, and days of colorful casts. The usual trips to the hospital at six o'clock in the morning continued for her appointments. As time passed, a feeling of joy and hope for everyone increased as we approached to the end of her treatment.

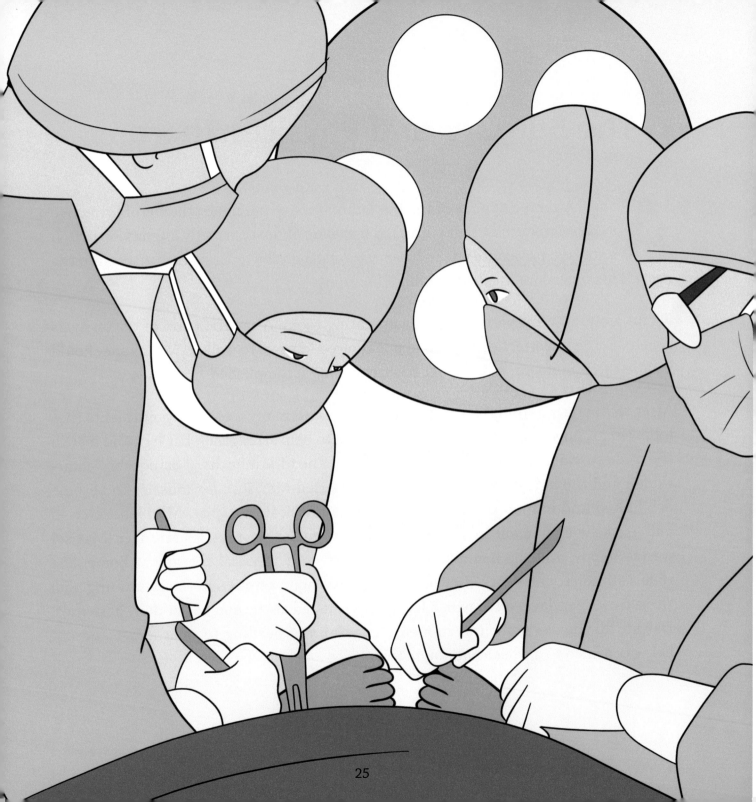

25

The Surgery and Physical Therapy

At last! After ten months of anxious and exhausted moments, the day of corrective surgery arrived! At that point, her feet were almost perfectly aligned, although a surgical procedure was necessary to lengthen the tendons that insert into the heels. This procedure is called Achilles Tenotomy.

Fortunately, all went perfectly in the operating room. A terrific team of doctors was able to fix the imperfections that had not allowed Marisol to walk as well as she should have. At that moment, most of her treatment was accomplished.

After recuperating from the surgery, there were still many weekly appointments that followed for physical therapy. This was needed to help strengthen her legs and feet so she could sustain herself in a standing position. The nine months of being wheelchair-ridden and the lack of physical activity had caused Marisol's leg muscles to become debilitated and immobile. Under the care of a physical therapist, Marisol exercised and used the equipment in the hospital gym to make her muscles stronger. Marisol was so happy, and she had much fun with her daily physical therapy at home. She rode a stationary bike for thirty minutes and did aqua aerobics in the swimming pool three times per day—all of which left her exhausted at the end of her daily activities. Despite all the work, she was immensely joyful, not needing to wear a cast and not being confined to a wheelchair anymore.

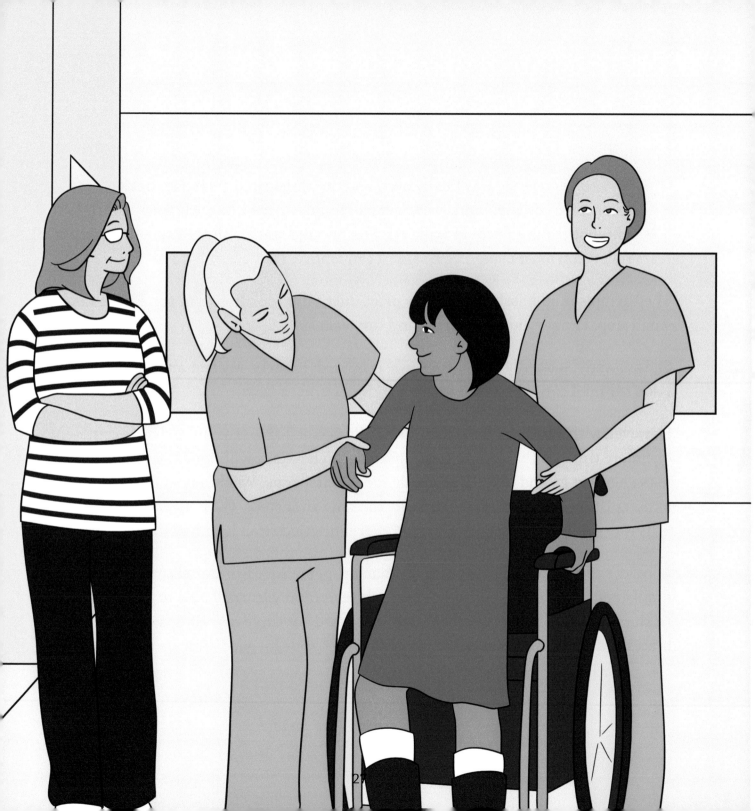

The recovery period was finally over, and the anticipated great day to take her very first steps with her brand-new feet had finally arrived. She was terrified, and she did not think she could walk yet. She became static and frightened. A river of tears rolled down her cheeks. She said, "I can't move. I'm not going to be able to walk."

The therapist and I assured her. "It's okay. Just take your time and try. Please take a small step. I know you are so brave and can walk."

She answered tearfully, "No, no, I can't. It is hard. It hurts. My feet are going to break. I don't think I can take a step yet."

However, with lots of patience, she was finally persuaded to trust us and to be confident one more time. At that point, it was up to her to have the willingness and strength to make her feet go and to walk normally for the first time. Wobbling, and supported by a therapist on each side, she eventually took her first steps. *What a miracle!* I thought. This was surely a blessing for all of us. Everyone cried from happiness!

Marisol's courage was outstanding. With many persuasive words and support from her family and friends who encouraged her, she eventually learned how to walk properly. At the final stage of her treatment, she welcomed her three new companions: a pair of braces and two fine pink crutches, which were set aside for good after six months of use.

29

Marisol Returns Home with Her New Feet

With her treatment finally completed, Marisol's feet were measured. She was so excited to go shopping for many different pairs of shoes to take home. Her favorite footwear were sandals, which she had never been able to wear properly before. Brand-new feet, now brand-new shoes. One had never seen a girl so happy and grateful.

Finally, time also arrived for to me to fly to Bolivia and return Marisol to her family, the home where she belonged. The two of us went through incredibly sad parting moments because of the close bond we had formed throughout her medical treatment.

* * *

Concluding Remark

I have watched and admired Marisol's struggles over the years, and every time, I have realized that Marisol is a strong and amazing little girl who will go far in this world. Mostly, I am proud because she was able to overcome an adversity in her life. Today Marisol is a happy teenager, dancing and enjoying her teenage years. Her dream and future endeavors are to graduate from high school, to study medicine, and eventually become an orthopedic surgeon and to help other special-needs children.

Repeatedly, my gratitude is immensely sealed forever to the doctors and medical assistants for their accomplishments—likewise, to all our dear friends and the clubs that gave their care, time, and financial support unselfishly.

Printed in the United States
by Baker & Taylor Publisher Services